THIS NOTEBOOK BELONGS TO

CONTACT

See our range of fine, illustrated books, ebooks, notebooks and art calendars:
www.flametreepublishing.com

This is a **FLAME TREE NOTEBOOK**
Published and © copyright 2021 Flame Tree Publishing Ltd

FTPB 104 • 978-1-78755-838-0

MOOMIN

Cover image based on a detail from
Moomin and Snorkmaiden from *Finn Family Moomintroll*
by Tove Jansson (1914–2001)
© Moomin Characters™

Tove Jansson was a Finnish-Swedish writer and artist who created
the Moomin family and their friends. She first started painting
Moomintrolls in 1935 and her last Moomin book was published
in 1970; but her stories live on and continue to be adapted and
enjoyed by many generations.

FLAME TREE PUBLISHING | The Art of Fine Gifts
6 Melbray Mews, London SW6 3NS, United Kingdom